Why Should a Child Be Born?

Why Should a Child Be Born?

Poems for Peace and Justice in the Middle East

S T Kimbrough, Jr.

Foreword by
James H. Charlesworth

RESOURCE *Publications* · Eugene, Oregon

WHY SHOULD A CHILD BE BORN?
Poems for Peace and Justice in the Middle East

Resource Publications
An Imprint of Wipf and Stock Publishers
199 W. 8th Ave., Suite 3
Eugene, OR 97401

www.wipfandstock.com

PAPERBACK ISBN: 978-1-5326-4369-9
HARDCOVER ISBN: 978-1-5326-4370-5
EBOOK ISBN: 978-1-5326-4371-2

Manufactured in the U.S.A.

Note from the author: The plea of these poems is that the adherents of the three Abrahamic faiths of the Middle East—Jews, Christians, and Muslims—in the midst of conflicts that have precipitated the persecution, starvation, and death of thousands, particularly children, acknowledge their common humanity and work together for peace and harmony.

"Poetry is thoughts that breathe, and words that burn."

THOMAS GRAY, *SELECTED POEMS*

Contents

Contents

Contents

Foreword

Who Is Hearing the Tolling Knell of Parting Day?

MY LONG-TIME FRIEND, S T Kimbrough, Jr., asks: "Why should a child be born into the world today?" I often heard that question when I was a professor at Duke in the 1960s. But that was a more naïve time, and the state of the world is appreciably less hopeful for tomorrow. Too many of my contacts would agree with the author of *4 Ezra* who reported a vision that the world to come will bring torments to many (7:47).

Kimbrough, esteemed Charles Wesley scholar and baritone of the Bonn Opera (Germany) and other European theaters, has also asked me to write an introduction to his collection of poems. I am very pleased to do so, having lived with Kurdish, Arab, Palestinian, Israeli, Syrian, Jordanian, Gazan, Egyptian, and Ethiopian children. My eyes have been haunted forever by their eyes that were repeatedly drained of hope. My ears ring with the screams that crescendo incessantly, penetrating down into the otherwise inaccessible regions of my being. I do hope my introduction to these timely poems will provide the context for many of them.

As I write these reflections, I remember a Kurdish boy of about five whom I inadvertently insulted while I was too focused on searching for the lost library of the Nestorians in southeast Turkey near Iran and Iraq. He entered the little tent city in which a former astronaut I had chosen was base commander. We looked to him like aliens, tall and well fed. He looked up to me and raised his hands, then opened them. He was offering me the tiny eggs from a bird's nest he had found while climbing precariously in the high cliffs. Why didn't I bend down, accept his gift, and show love for the disguised little drummer boy? Though unseen, I recognize him in Kimbrough's words:

If I were in a gentler mood,
perhaps I'd be more wise and good.

I still hear the penetrating shrieks of an Arab boy directly beneath me as I sat on the veranda of the faculty club on Mount Scopus where Titus stationed his troops as he began to destroy Jerusalem. I have never heard such earth-splitting screams. Why was the boy pouring out his guts? Had his father been arrested and taken to a prison? Why were the shouts unremitting? He was not hurt; he was annihilated. Kimbrough heard such screams:

In Israel and Palestine
some have forgotten charity,
a brutal fact that I opine:
a land devoid of parity.

I still see the filthy face of a little Palestinian boy of about one whose face was covered with flies as he sat forlorn on a street near the *via dolorosa* and within the walls of Old Jerusalem. The black flies landed on his nose, encircled his face, and made numerous trips to warm piles of donkey fecal refuse to his left. No one seemed to care. He sat alone, rejected, noticed only by filthy flies. Kimbrough feels the abandoned child in Abraham's lot:

Yet Christians, Jews, and Muslims
of God-created birth
cannot ignore the problems
that decrease their faith's worth.

Sitting in my office in Ramat haSharon, in northern Tel Aviv, I frequently ran down the stairs when I heard sirens of a rocket coming toward me. In the stairwell, I heard a loud explosion. Then, returning to my office, I looked out the window and saw two vapor trails. Then I experienced the fears of the little children in the Negev, near Gaza, terrorized by the many rockets for decades that were aimed at them and their schools and homes. For years many a child awoke with stained sheets and developed nervous twitches. Why did no one notice … or noted but ignored? Such war-torn areas here in the Middle East shape the thoughts of Kimbrough's poetry:

O little town of Bethlehem,
no longer still you lie.
There is no deep and dreamless sleep,
for jets now fill the sky.

When I was in Damascus, I saw many children. Then they were happy and had many friends and frequented restaurants in which to enjoy life and food. Now all is rubble. Where are the children now? We know. None of us can forget that war-stained little boy in Syria sitting before the cameras. He was apparently all that was left from a very proud city that has a distinguished past. He looked straight ahead; his eyes were dead. Kimbrough wrote of Aleppo's children:

> Is there no sense of mercy left
> to spare the children who're bereft
> of every decent human need,
> because of power-grabbing greed?

Petra in Jordan is known as the rose-red city as old as time; but actually, the monumental structures there, built in living rock, are 2,000 years old, dating from the time of Hillel and Jesus. I can still see the smiling faces of little children—running—eager to impress me and show me what they had found or sell me something. I remember their unwashed faces and piercing dark eyes that never could twinkle with images of Tinker Bell. They knew I was a foreigner from another, mysterious country. Theirs was defined by tight borders, poverty, and limited resources. They knew they had no attractive futures. They ate pita bread, no pizza or hamburger. They drank tea, no chocolate milkshake. They washed by springs, no showers. They would not be educated but would waste their youthful fragrance on the desert air. Far more fortunate than the Kurdish, Gazan, Egyptian, and Ethiopian children who left lasting impressions on me, these Bedouin children could not imagine a country defined by trees full of bananas, oranges, and coconuts, like the Florida of my youth and like "the Paradise of Delight" created before the world (4 Ez 3:6 and 7:37). All children need and deserve love.

> Whose child is this? I ask,
> a child you've never known?
> Is it too great a task
> to love him as your own?

Being driven through Gaza in a taxi with all windows open and foul air wafting inside, I saw carts with produce sloshing away in a crowded market way whose surface consisted of a mixture of blood, mud, and feces from donkeys, camels, and horses. To my right was a baby boy of less than two. He was naked. He began to make his way from one side to the other of the unfordable river of slime. I could not see his face. He was trying his best, but the engulfing concoction was about to consume him. The taxi moved on and I lost sight of him. Was he born only to become part of the most despicable roadway imaginable? I see him dimly in these lines:

> A little boy stands parentless,
> but this he does not know;
> he last recalls his mother's cry—
> "I'll never let you go."

I cannot forget the little children less than eight years old slaving in a factory south of Cairo. They were making silk rugs to sell; one little boy of about three looked at me and smiled and then proudly demonstrated how hard he could work. Were they ostensibly incarcerated? Those outside without food and draped with rags dreamed of a decent clean place in which they also could find some work. I was assured that the chosen few would be given some education; was that a self-serving defense for child labor? Kimbrough encapsulates the poignancy:

> Every child of God's creation
> needs much more than deprivation
> to fulfill a life of dreams;
> food and nurture, love and caring,
> and to know each one is sharing
> in a life devoid of schemes.

North of Addis Ababa, in the mountains, I recall a young boy coming to me where I sat alone, trying to finish supper in the courtyard of a dilapidated hotel. He told me he needed money to get an education. He stood before me. I could see him shaking. I offered him a fifty-dollar bill. Was I the only savior he could imagine? Boys and girls came running to see me off in an old bus. They were abandoned by relatives and accompanied only by poverty, the elegant stones of a once proud culture, crimes from too many wars. The following poetry was shaped by such scenes:

> With energy, his lips he pressed
> 'gainst hers, breathed out, her lungs were stressed;
> till suddenly life's surging force
> evoked a scream of death's divorce,
> for she would live though badly maimed,
> while one more war crime goes unnamed.

All these children were and remain anonymous. If I saw any one of them in a list of three I could not identify him or her. Yet, their faces intermittently pop up before me as I reminisce about the many children that are brought into this world and are abandoned. Each of us has seen too many of them in the televised evening news for about fifty years; most of us remember the little girl dressed in red while all others moved in grey zones in a film on the holocaust by Spielberg called *Schindler's List*. She ran with panic without direction and was last seen piled like refuse on a wheelbarrow.

Apparently still with the smoke of the burning flesh from the Temple in his nostrils, the Jewish author of 4 Ezra announces that it would have been better if Adam had not been created (7:46[116]). The apocalyptist had seen Titus' troops burn Jerusalem and murder priests as they continued to worship in the Temple; and he stood helpless as he saw thousands of little children rounded up and sold as slaves. Yes, Adam, it would have been better if you had not lived; for you had an evil heart that we all have inherited from you (3:20; 7:48).

During the Black Plague, John Donne composed words many of us have memorized: "Do not ask for whom the bell tolls. It tolls for thee." Indeed, we should not have forgotten that every one's death diminishes me. Thomas Gray metaphorically viewed the curfew of parting day and left us imagining how the plowman homeward plods his weary way, leaving the world to darkness. The children! How many were precious gems hidden in the dark caves of the unfathomable ocean? How many were flowers who wasted their fragrance on the desert air?

Do humans have a future? If so, is it going to be a nightmare as depicted in Animal Farm and too many movies about a post-third-world-war rubble? Einstein was right that the next war would not be like the previous wars; it would annihilate all human cultures. After it a war will be fought like the first one with sticks and stones. Again, I recall a lament of the author of 4 Ezra: "O Adam, what have you done? For though it was you who sinned, the fall was not yours alone, but ours also who are your descendants" (7:48[118]).[1]

In his letters, Albert Schweitzer mentioned to Einstein and others that the foundation of all morality is a reverence for life. He meant all life. When he killed a mosquito, it was to stop the malaria that was killing his patients.

---

1. Bruce Metzger in The Old Testament Pseudepigrapha. Ed. James H. Charlesworth. 2 vols. (1983, 1985), 1:541.

What if we do not learn to think and act according to Schweitzer's perspicacious insight? Life would be marginalized and robots with abilities superior to ours, because we designed them that way, would be more valuable than any living being. That would make a travesty of biblical truths. If we learn to indwell with all our being Schweitzer's "reverence for life," humanity has a future, and wise and informed tolerance will be our helmsman. Can we upright the sinking ship of a culture once proud of its belief that all are created equal with inalienable rights? We all are immigrants from some land or some icy comet; but are we still yearning to be free and sharing that perspective with all others?

Will we all be dressed in red, perhaps stained by our own blood, and discarded in a garbage pile never to be excavated since humanity killed itself? Are we living in a relatively peaceful time zone in which we manage to eke out each day between the World Depression, World War II, the Holocaust, and the rule of those suicide bombers who obliterate with unimaginable pain more than they can imagine?

Kimbrough's poetic reflections bring into focus what is seen only in a mirror dimly. Children are defenseless. They need mothers, fathers, and family. Sane people still inhabit our globe; by reading Kimbrough's words all of them will feel motivated to help all children, especially those in our own neighborhoods.

Kimbrough's poetry frames the picture that filters to us usually through the television. I have seen it up close, face to face. Let us never forget the suffering that defines our world and our lives. If prayer is efficacious, let us pray that our thoughts and sacrificing actions will help "thy kingdom come on earth as it is in heaven." That dream has the tradition and power to unite Jews, Christians, and Muslims.

James H. Charlesworth,
Professor of New Testament Language and Literature
Princeton Theological Seminary
Princeton, NJ

Acknowledgments

THE AUTHOR EXPRESSES DEEPEST appreciation to Dr. J. Richard Watson, Emeritus Professor of English of the University of Durham (UK) for his careful reading of these poems and his thoughtful suggestions, and to Charles A. Green for his judicious reading of the manuscript. Also, gratitude is due Dr. James H. Charlesworth, friend, colleague, Dead Sea Scroll scholar, savant of ancient Middle East history, and an advocate of peace, justice, and understanding among all peoples for his eye-opening Foreword.

Section 1

Children

1. Why Should a Child Be Born?

Why should a child be born
    into the world today?
Why should its life be torn
    amid the human fray?
A child is born to love,
    to cuddle and caress,
for cooing like the dove;
    it is not born for stress.

Why should a child be born
    to suffer amid war?
Why should it be forlorn
    and ask, "What is life for?"
Why should it suffer death
    for others' power and greed?
It tells you with each breath:
    "Love, love is what I need!"

Why should a child have pain
    from hateful blows and strife?
Why should life seem insane?
    Each child wants loving life.
Why should then child abuse
    go on without an end?
For this there's no excuse,
    each child's your loving friend.

Why should a child be born
    into the world today?
We are indeed forlorn
    unless we hear it say:
"I come to bring you joy,
    love, laughter, hope, and peace.
I am a girl, a boy;
    So love me, love me, please!"

2. Children of Creation

In this world it is essential
to pursue each child's potential
    with every means at hand.
This should never be an option,
but a mandate for adoption
    in every clime and land.

Yet with warring and with killing;
Who will show that they are willing
    to explain what *human* means?
All are children of creation
filled with growing expectation
    which to good or evil leans.

Every child-born expectation
can be smothered by starvation
    and eclipsed by hunger pains.
Poverty can stifle learning
and destroy all childhood yearning
    till all expectation wanes.

Every child of God's creation
needs much more than deprivation
    to fulfill a life of dreams;
food and nurture, love and caring,
and to know each one is sharing
    in a life devoid of schemes.

Love's the highest expectation
of each child in every nation;
    never mind the race or creed.
Fulfill now the intervention
of the true, divine intention:
    love a child, life's noblest deed.

3. War's Martyred Children

A city filled with martyrs' blood—
Aleppo's children face the flood
of violent, murderous onslaught
of bombs that turn their lives to naught.
They're injured, starved, and left for dead
without a place to lay their head.

One cries out, "Stop!" and "Be humane!"
A child should never die in vain!
Each child dies martyred for no cause,
war's victim without any pause
of senseless rulers' selfish pride,
their ego never put aside.

Instead they terrify each child;
without a care they are reviled!
Is there no sense of mercy left
to spare the children who're bereft
of every decent human need,
because of power-grabbing greed?

Wake up, you senseless thieves of war,
no longer spread your lawless lore:
"It matters not who dies today,
as long as I can have my way."
Each child, who dies and lacks for bread,
dies with its blood upon your head!

4. The Children of War's Misery

The children of war's misery
who now their own affliction see
    and hunger daily know,
wait patiently, nothing receive,
in suffering and in sorrow live;
    their faces marked by woe.

Are these but temporal sufferings here,
to which the world turns a deaf ear?
    Too late, yes, it's too late!
For some must live and some must die,
we need not know the reason why—
    a necessary fate.

Alas, this fatalistic view
is limited to just a few
    but traps the minds of those
who care not for each child that's born,
lest curse of war leave them forlorn
    in misery's sad throes.

Shall we sit by, in secret mourn,
and wait for hearts to be reborn
    and kindness, mercy show?
If this we do, we play the fool,
become a fatalistic tool
    that helps no child to grow.

Each child needs love and nurture *now*
with every human being's vow:
    Each child will live and grow!
No war, disaster shall deprive
the fight to keep each child alive;
    our love each day they'll know.

5. One More War Crime!

The laughter of a child of three
made hearts o'erflow as spirits free.
Her brothers thought she was a charm
and danced her round from arm to arm.
They sang with joy and such delight
till neighbors joined the rapturous sight.
Then suddenly the ground did shake,
her eyes and mouth began to ache.
The stench was stifling from the gas,
a bomb dropped with a "copter" pass.
The little girl's chest lurched for breath,
her brothers all had met their death.
Her swollen cheeks with blood were red;
an elder man now held her head.
With energy, his lips he pressed
'gainst hers, breathed out, her lungs were stressed;
till suddenly life's surging force
evoked a scream of death's divorce,
for she would live though badly maimed,
while one more war crime goes unnamed.

6. A Gaza Playground

The wind blew freshly
across the children's faces
as they gathered to play.
"Hide and seek" was again their choice,
but their playground now was changed.
Uncle Ahmed's house reduced to rubble
could not be their starting point.
The schoolhouse was no longer there—
just mangled steel and stone.
As far as they could see
their playground loomed before them
like a twisted colossus
of bent metal and shattered cement.
Still, the children laughed,
and a little girl said, "Let's play!"
There were just five of them.
Four would run to hide, and
the eldest would start the search.
He covered his eyes
and they scattered like flies,
leaping over jagged steel and stones.
They grinned and smiled,
crawling into bombed-out spaces,
hoping not to be found.
One scratched an elbow,
another tore her dress,
while another cut his hand.
Still they happily played on
for this was the only playground
that was left.

7. Whose Child Is This?

Whose child is this? I ask,
    a child you've never known?
Is it too great a task
    to love him as your own?
With food and shelter, tender care,
a healing touch, and clothes to wear—
with outstretched arms, will you be there?
Refrain:
    Each child is God's child, yours, and mine—
    You are a gift of love divine.

Whose child is this? I see
    a child you've always known.
How strange it is to me—
    you've left her all alone!
In summer, autumn, winter, spring
you never thought—What shall I bring
to make her lonely spirit sing?
Refrain

Whose child is this—black, red,
    white, yellow, bronze, or brown,
born without racists' dread
    or prejudicial frown?
Why teach a child hate, violence, greed,
and violate the Maker's creed?—
Through love, God's love, the world is freed!
Refrain

8. Help the Children

Why are children so ignored
    by politicians' claims
that they know what's best for all,
    and focus on their names?

Because their own reflections
    are *the* important thing!
They focus on elections,
    while to their posts they cling?

The children starving daily,
    in lands ravaged by war,
cannot cast a vote for them.
    Help children now? What for?

Can human nature blindly
    ignore a starving child?
Yes, politicians' egos
    let hunger oft run wild.

It matters not if wild storms,
    or raging war's vast waste
leave children suffering, hungering!
    Will no one act with haste?

Section 2

Refugees

9. The Plight of Refugees

Who on this earth can comprehend
    the plight of refugees?
They're stripped of human dignity
    and brought down to their knees.
Their homes destroyed and destitute,
    they struggle to escape
the horrors of their daily lives—
    violence, death, and rape.

A little boy stands parentless,
    but this he does not know;
he last recalls his mother's cry—
    "I'll never let you go."
The blast that tore him from her breast
    baptized him with her blood;
and on the ground right next to him
    are shoes where once she stood.

So stunned he cannot cry for help,
    he stares with empty gaze,
emotionless and motionless,
    entranced as in a daze.
Before more blasts can frighten him,
    a trembling outstretched arm
embraces him with tenderness
    as if to shield from harm.

It is his sister who survived
    and holds him close and tight;
her dress is torn, in shreds she stands,
    her eyes are pierced with fright.
As quickly as sharp lightning bolts
    a crowd had huddled round
and covered both the girl and boy
    and laid them on the ground.

Another barrel bomb might strike
    as swiftly as the first,
but silence reigned like death itself;
    the atmosphere seemed cursed.
The minutes seemed like crawling hours
    and then all rose to flee;
the smoke was thick as molten ash;
    they tried but could not see.

Just then the driver of a truck
    cried, "Are you friend or foe?"
"Friend," all of them with anguish screamed;
    "Climb on, we have to go!"
They drove for hours through mud and rain,
    the shelling never ceased;
the boy and girl sat holding hands,
    as fear and fright increased.

Just as the border came in view
    The truck would lurch. then balk.
The driver yelled—"Our petrol's gone!
    Get out, you'll have to walk."
By dead of night they could not see
    the jagged, dark terrain;
they fell and cut their hands and arms
    but had no time for pain.

The fear of being caught once more
    by angry, ruthless men,
drove them on like violent wind—
    They thought, "No! Not again!"
Just then a border guard cried out,
    "Who are you? Who goes there?"
With fear they trembled, could not speak.
    Was this another snare?

A blinding light flashed face on face,
 each countenance aghast.
Was this their fate—to be turned back?
 Were they not safe at last?
The border guard said, "Come this way,
 we're going to let you through.
The camp for refugees is full;
 we'll find a place for you."

He showed them space between two tents:
 "It's all that can be found,"
were the last words they heard him say,
 as they lay on the ground.
The night was desperately cold,
 their bodies racked with chill.
When daylight broke, another day
 had dawned to test their will.

10. The Fear of Refugees

What do we fear in refugees—
    their language, culture, creed?
Their reverence, praying on their knees,
    or language we can't read?

Or do we fear the smell of food
    we've never smelled before?
Or gestures that to us seem rude,
    strange clothes we see next door?

Above all, is there the concern—
    they think not as we think,
without ability to earn,
    will *our* finances shrink?

America, our history
    is one of refugees,
and it is not a mystery
    they came, and land did seize.

Their languages not unified,
    from Germany, France, Spain,
and England too: no one denied
    the chance to grasp terrain.

Though native nations they subdued,
    their languages unknown,
they claimed a right they had pursued:
    a land to call their own.

The native nations had no chance
    against invading bands
of refugees, the soldier's lance;
    they died by foreign hands.

Our land was built by refugees
    who turned against their past,
forsook their nationalities
    and then the die was cast:

Created equal all are we,
    all have the right to life,
pursuit of happiness is free,
    though not devoid of strife.

May refugees today expect
    this kind of guarantee;
or have our freedoms all been wrecked
    "from sea to shining sea"?

11. Who Are They?

What mean, rapacious folk are they
who turn the refugees away?
They eat their fill both day and night
and want the needy out of sight.

What crass, malicious folk are they
who turn the refugees away?
"They'll change our culture and our creed!
It matters not if they are freed!"

What foul, capricious folk are they
who turn the refugees away?
They claim their freedom to defend,
while others' liberty they spend.

What cold, pernicious folk are they
who turn the refugees away?
Their sly deception traps each soul
and shrouds with death the lives they stole.

12. One Refugee's Story

Afghanistan he fled with haste;
    his house was bombed, his wife was killed.
A journalist, he'd plied his trade,
    his articles with truth were filled.
Homeless, alone, and on the run,
    he never thought that this could be.
Such stories he had often told,
    but now *he* was the refugee.

He'd studied years before abroad,
    English and French he'd learned quite well.
But studies in no way prepared
    to help him march his way through hell.
Where could he go, who'd take him in?
    "Perhaps I'll test my fate in France.
If I can possibly get there,
    the language will be my best chance."

He'd worked as an interpreter
    for U.S. forces' top command.
This marked him as an enemy.
    Could he now evil threats withstand?
His ID papers blown to bits,
    he had no passport, thus no name.
No one will take him at his word?
    They'll laugh and tell him he's to blame.

For all the money he had left
    a smuggler's truck took him to Greece,
but dumped him out when someone screamed,
    "Stop now! Stop now! We're the police!"
They left him in a dark, dank camp
    with other desperate refugees.
Now months have passed, and he's lost hope
    and sick from stench of beds with fleas.

Each day he tries to tell someone,
    "I'm wise, well taught, can be of use,"
But prejudice is so widespread,
    that refugees know but abuse.
"I speak three languages, what's more,
    a journalist and I can write."
"But you've no passport!" still they say,
    "It's best we send you back tonight!"

13. Grieve and Grieve

Where can we sleep tonight, Papa?
    I was so cold last night.
I had no blanket or pillow
    from dusk until daylight.

We always had a fire at home
    to keep us all so warm.
Why did they bomb and tear it down?
    We did not do them harm.

And then we had to run away;
    no one would help us out.
Why were those men with guns so mean?
    "Run, run," I heard you shout!

My mother took me by the hand
    I heard her loudly scream,
"Son, run! for we have no more time;
    the crater's spewing steam!"

We ran and ran, we were so tired,
    I fell and cut my arm.
There was no time to stop the blood,
    which filled me with alarm.

We found our neighbors, who had fled;
    their house had been bombed too.
They'd found a camp where they could stay,
    and said, "We've room for you."

The snow was falling round their tent,
    a fierce wind howled and blew.
I wondered if another night,
    somehow we'd make it through.

My mother held me to her breast;
    her body felt so warm.
Outside the wind and blizzard raged,
    a fierce, breathtaking storm.

Would we have food at morning's light?
    Would we then have to leave?
We have no winter clothes for warmth;
    must we just grieve and grieve?

What will befall our family?
    We have no place to go!
War's made us orphans one and all,
    our fate is woe on woe!

14. O Syria, O Syria

O Syria, O Syria,
    we mourn your tragic fate:
cities destroyed, thousands have fled,
    and hearts are racked with hate.

Where Sunni, Shia, Alawites
    lived decades side by side,
divisions deep have led to scorn,
    and harmony has died.

Along Aleppo's empty streets
    a starving child walks by,
then searches through a garbage heap,
    while muffling its own cry.

Rank chaos reigns throughout the land
    with factions so profuse—
yet freedom fighters, Syrian troops
    shirk peace without excuse.

A Syrian diaspora
    spans Europe and Mid-East;
and millions are now refugees
    but are they free at least?

They're doctors, lawyers, merchants too
    without a home or land
and children who will never know
    the home from which they're banned.

Some lie in squalor of tent camps
    in Europe's vast expanse,
awaiting mercy and good will—
    but will they have a chance?

Section 3

The Holy Land?

15. Why Should We Call It "Holy"?

Why should we call it "Holy"—
    the land of three great faiths—
when war in this "Holy Land"
    makes these religions wraiths?
Yes, ghosts of themselves they are:
    "Thou shalt not kill" is lost
amid the clamor to spar
    for land at any cost.

Yet Christians, Jews, and Muslims
    of God-created birth,
cannot ignore the problems
    that decrease their faith's worth.
Who says, "Love your enemies"?
    Who says, "Love your neighbor"?
These virtues of behavior
    are a long-lost labor.

Who'll dare to reclaim "Holy,"
    a word that justly claims
Israel/Palestine indeed
    birthed faiths with sacred aims?
Will they to their roots return
    and there find holy strength,
rewrite our modern history
    with days of truth-sought length?

Luke 19:41–42, "As he came near and saw the city, he wept over it, saying, 'If you, even you, had only recognized on this day the things that make for peace! But now they are hidden from your eyes.'"

16. Jerusalem, Jerusalem

Jerusalem, Jerusalem,
    of three faiths, the holy seat:
What have the faithful made of them—
    turned faithfulness to deceit?
These Abrahamic faiths all speak
    of dignity, love, respect,
and bid God's creatures to be meek,
    one asks, "But to what effect?"

A history full of turmoil,
    the skyline tells the story
of those who claimed you as their spoil
    and thought they brought you glory.
A synagogue, a steepled cross,
    a majestic golden dome,
are symbols of the gain and loss
    of a place someone calls home.

Jerusalem, Jerusalem,
    for you we weep, pray, and mourn,
from you hope of the world should stem,
    from you peace should be reborn.
Where are the faithful who will say,
    "Each soul's worth more than a cause!"
Shall our divisions have their way—
    a stalemate of human flaws?

No wall or border can exclude
    God's people born to be free,
but harmony, peace they delude
    with deceptive certainty.

Jerusalem, Jerusalem,
    we pray, we pray for your peace,
for force and violence condemn
    hope upon hope, to decrease.

Will no one break this damning chain—
    endless inhumanity?
Relieve the suffering and the pain
    caused by sheer insanity?
Your ancient prophets plead for peace:
    Turn swords to plows for the land!
Let justice reign and violence cease!
    The time for just peace is at hand!

17. No Charity, No Parity

In Israel and Palestine
  some have forgotten charity,
a brutal fact that I opine:
  a land devoid of parity.
They plunder land to be secure
  or so the self-righteous proclaim,
and view their action just and pure—
  a promise in God's holy name.

While taking land from town to town,
  forgotten is Amos of old:
"Let justice roll like waters down!"
  and seekers of justice be bold!
No charity, no equal rights,
  no parity or equal pay!
One waits and waits for days and nights,
  while all one can do is to pray.

Prayers in a Mosque or synagogue,
  are they heard by the self-same God?
Or is one's God a demagogue,
  promoting political fraud?
Are we not all one humankind,
  beginning our lives as a child?
Should each child's purpose be maligned
  by hatred, crime, and greed run wild?

If every child knows only hate
  and sees in others only greed,
there is no way one can abate:
  "*I'm right! I alone!*" as a creed.
All children are not born with hate;
  it comes not by nature, it's taught.
Teach love of all or it's too late,
  and their lives will be lived for naught.

18. The Olive Tree

The way an olive tree
looked down on me,
its green-leafed branches
swaying as if to say,
"I have a tale
of ancient Palestine
my conquerors never knew"—
haunts my every thought.
"The Turks, the British,
Israelis too
did not want to know
the truth about my birth
or that I have a soul.
They only victoriously
shouted, 'They're mine—
that tree and land!'
If only they had taken time
to learn about my birth:
Centuries ago
a little boy knelt
at his father's feet,
and with his hands
pushed wide the earth
and made a space for me.
Then in an act of sacredness
he gently placed me there.
He bowed and whispered
tenderly, '*Salaam*, little
seedling, flourish and grow.'
Just then my soul, *salaam*—
shalom was born—*peace, peace,
my soul* was born.
If only those who said,
'They're mine,' would come

to know the truth:
an olive tree has a soul;
it is peace! True peace
they then will know."

19. "Subtle" Apartheid?

Apartheid has a color link,
at least that's what some people think!

White, yellow, black or red, or brown,
one color oft evokes a frown.

What if no color is assigned
and innocents are still maligned.

In Israel there's no color, hue,
used as an ethnic "who is who."

A Palestinian has no hue
that is distinct from every Jew.

How "subtle" can apartheid work?—
in Israel with a clever quirk.

The walls, restrictions, check points too
give the oppressors all their due.

They know that Jews all have a choice
to travel freely, with free voice.

But Palestinian's are not free,
even food and aid are blocked by sea.

Today apartheid's "subtle" yoke
in Israel is for "peace" a cloak.

This cloak of "peace" is but a show.
Justice is at an all-time low!

Apartheid "subtle" it is not!
Some live in ease, some are forgot!

20. Mourning for Bethlehem

O little town of Bethlehem,
  no longer still you lie.
There is no deep and dreamless sleep,
  for jets now fill the sky.
Now in your dark streets standing
  are walls that shut out light;
the hopes and fears of all the years
  aren't met in you tonight.

Though Christ was born of Mary,
  and gathered all above,
no mortals sleep, and soldiers keep
  no watch of wondering love.
Though morning stars together
  proclaimed the holy birth,
there is no song that we can sing,
  for there's no peace on earth.

Not silently, not silently
  the wondrous gift is driven
from human hearts though God imparts
  the blessings of his heaven.
We hear the constant outburst
  of bombs and dying souls.
Where is good will and peace on earth,
  for hate has no controls!

O holy Child of Bethlehem,
  descend to us we pray,
cast out our sin and enter in,
  be born in us today.
Instill the Christmas message
  of love, good will, and peace
in all on earth of every faith,
  that war and hatred cease.

Original poem by Phillip Brooks

O little town of Bethlehem,
  How still we see thee lie;
above thy deep and dreamless sleep
  The silent stars go by.
Yet in thy dark streets shineth
  the everlasting light;
the hopes and fears of all the years
  Are met in thee tonight.

For Christ is born of Mary,
  and gathered all above,
while mortals sleep, the angels keep
  their watch of wondering love.
O morning stars together,
  proclaim the holy birth,
and praises sing to God the King,
  And peace to men on earth!

How silently, how silently,
  the wondrous gift is given;
so God imparts to human hearts,
  The blessings of his heaven.
No ear may hear his coming,
  But in this world of sin,
where meek souls will receive him. Still
  The dear Christ enters in.

O holy Child of Bethlehem,
  descend to us we pray,
cast out our sin and enter in,
  Be born in us today.
We hear the Christmas angels
  the great glad tidings tell;
O come to us, abide with us,
  Our Lord Emmanuel.

21. The Christmas Bells of Bethlehem

The Christmas bells of Bethlehem
    ring once again for peace,
while soldiers, as at Jesus' birth,
    are "peace-making" police!
"We'll keep the peace no matter what!"
    Their oracle divine:
"You think one little child brings peace?
    Not so, it's *our* design!"

The Christmas bells of Bethlehem
    ring out: "Goodwill to all!"
No matter what one's faith or creed
    goodwill creates no wall.
Where shall we find acts of goodwill
    when bombs destroy a home,
when children die of gunshot wounds,
    and no one knows *Shalom*?

The Christmas bells of Bethlehem
    ring out, but who will hear?
Their message is consistently
    the same from year to year:
"A child brings peace, good will to earth."
    Yet this seems hard to learn!
A child, goodwill, and lasting peace—
    the world's yet to discern.

22. The Wall of Bethlehem

A wall now circles Bethlehem
    to keep the evil Arabs in.
Officials say, "It's us or them,
    so everyone we will condemn
to life behind the wall, secure.
    It matters not what dwellers say,
for Christians, Muslims there's no cure—
    Those living there our trust betray.

Yet life behind the wall goes on,
    children are born, they laugh and play.
For hope dies not with each new dawn;
    diversity has won the day!
A college now reveals the scene
    where all of any faith or creed
learn side by side, no wall between;
    of ethnic tests there is no need.

Perhaps the wall keeps evil out.
    The other side shows signs of hate,
of bigotry, of life in doubt,
    where settlers claims one can't negate.
How strange! They have a sacred book
    which says, "You shall not steal, defraud"!
Where now in Israel must one look
    for those whose views remain unflawed?

The wall officials sanctioned, built,
    offers no one security.
It only fosters guilt on guilt—
    a sign of immaturity.
The town the wall incarcerates
    once birthed a Child of Peace, Goodwill.
That peace no wall obliterates,
    Goodwill no wall can make stand still!

Build all the walls you wish, good friends,
    their destiny is not goodwill.
They hinder peace, its noble ends,
    its overtures most surely kill.
How laughable the petty thought—
    a wall makes life for all secure!
Goodwill and peace all must be taught
    or destiny is *never* sure!

23. The "Promised Land"?

What happened to the promise
of the "Promised Land"?
The promise to build homes,
to have children, to pray, and
to care for the neighbor?
Have the chosen people
chosen to be faithless?
The promised land has become
a land of racism and despotism,
a land of pain and brokenness—
the rich are richer,
the poor are poorer!
Must the oppressed cry, "Unclean!"
like the lepers of old—
so some will pity them?
Is pity all they need?
Did God promise to divide
the people of creation—
those who have and
those who have not?
No! God promised peace on earth
good will to all, and life abundant!
Only when this promise is fulfilled,
will the "Promised Land" truly be
the land of promise!

24. The Land of Promise

The land of promise, Palestine
    has such a stormy past,
a land of ancient city-states
    whose power could not last.

The Canaanites created them,
    the rivalries were fierce:
Lachish, Gezer, Jerusalem
    their strongest walls could pierce.

Then Israel with King David
    sought all to unify,
but separate, rival kingdoms
    it then could not deny.

The northern kingdom Israel
    'gainst southern Judah rose,
and God's supposed elected ones
    chose justice to oppose.

Assyrians, Babylonians
    invaded from the East
and both the kingdoms overran,
    the greatest to the least.

Now modern times the past repeat:
    the Turks and British too
have both waged war and thought they won,
    but peace was not in view.

Today the land of Israel
    is also waging war
and on the past of Palestine
    has quickly shut the door.

"Let justice like the streams run down,"[1]
    the prophet Amos said,
for Arabs, Israelis, for all—
    On others do not tread!

But modern Israel/Palestine
    ignores justice for all,
as though the prophet never spoke!
    No justice, but a wall!

There's wholesale, complete betrayal
    of Israel's sacred book,
for "Do not defraud your neighbor,"[2]
    Israel has forsook.

1. Amos 5:24.
2. Leviticus 19:13.

Section 4

War and Peace

25. Statistics from a War

Statistics from a war are cold.
    They're sterile, and the facts they tell
of souls who've daily met their death
    are garnered from a living hell.

How many children died last week?
    Did any parents yet survive?
An entire village was destroyed,
    no child or parent left alive.

O yes, one hundred bodies found.
    They're twenty little girls and boys
and forty men bound hands and feet.
    The rest were women raped for joys.

These so-called joys are ruthless acts
    of soldiers all who've mothers had.
The lifeless women all were raped
    by men whose mothers must be sad.

They nursed their sons with loving care
    and taught them what should matter most.
They did not teach to rape and kill!
    Of such things mothers do not boast.

One more statistic from a war:
    One hundred villagers are dead;
each one has just a number now.
    Would we had *known* them all instead!

26. Weapons of War

Weapons of war respect no one,
  though crafted by the keenest minds.
The brightest intellects have spun
  an art that sense and evil binds.

How sensible the ancient thought:
  "By power and might others to rule!"
Even arrows, spears, in their day brought
  refining crafts warfare to fuel.

But now they seem so obsolete;
  instead of killing one by one
the modern bombs bring swift defeat,
  surpassing Attila the Hun.

Refined though modern weapons be,
  the scourge of death remains the same:
the gurgling gasp of one's last breath—
  the art of weapons' deadly aim.

How inhumane this human art,
  perfected, sharpened, and refined
to crush the gift, tear it apart:
  the greatest gift, the human mind.

Drop one more bomb of malice, hate;
  send deadly missiles through the sky.
Destroy all hope, this is our fate,
  war's weapons cannot answer, "Why?"

27. Hate

"Hate," the word, has letters four
  which no one stops to spell
before showing its manners
  on paths that lead to hell.
Short of its curse no one stops
  who acts the Satan part,
but drives the hatred arrow
  right through the human heart.

There is no simple answer
  for the dread curse of hate,
but once you have been taught it
  perhaps it is too late;
too late to change your language,
  to rid it of uncouth,
troubling words like "Coon" or "Chink"
  you've spoken from your youth.

You learned the ways so quickly,
  even when you did not know,
when looks were smirked or laughed at,
  and it was done for show.
You stood by laughing coldly
  as if you half approved.
How swiftly your thoughtfulness
  for others was removed!

But hate soon grows to hate crimes,
  that denigrate and kill!
The art of being human
  is humankind's lost skill!
A star, a cross, a swastika
  are signs employed to brand
the hateful acts of violence
  within one's own homeland.

As surely as the sun sets,
    the moon glows in the night,
somewhere there's hatred brewing,
    denying someone's right
to happiness and justice,
    to peace and solitude,
till all is ruled by hatred
    and moral turpitude.

Can there be no redemption
    from evil hate's morass?
Can we not unlearn hatred?
    Must hate on hate amass?
The hope is this: to show love
    to those we think to hate.
Start now with all the children—
    let friendship be their fate!

28. Hate and Exclusivity

Hate and exclusivity
    are paramount to those
with a strong proclivity
    all tolerance to oppose.

Intense dislike for others
    the hateful gladly choose;
their hate all kindness smothers,
    while others they abuse.

Open minds and open thought
    risk violence, disdain,
for hatred is with vice fraught—
    with lies, an endless skein.

Hatred is a dead-end street:
    no reason and no sense;
its destiny—sure defeat;
    its purpose—no defense.

Hate the skin not like your own,
    hate others' beliefs too:
Everything but hate disown;
    some will believe it true.

Hate dresses oft in fatigues,
    in swastikas and boots,
and plots shameful, bold intrigues,
    and creates vile disputes.

It lurks behind a settler's gun,
    a belt that holds a bomb;
it kills before a child can run,
    no matter where she's from.

If hate would be deleted
    from every human mind,
then tolerance would be greeted
    with love that's intertwined.

29. Damascus

Damascus, vast ancient city,
    an architectural dream
of storied structures, manuscripts,
    an endless cultural stream.

Your tribes and many languages,
    your trading caravans,
made you an ethnic melting pot
    of folk from many lands.

The commerce and the intellect
    which bloomed within your gates
made you the envy of the East
    and hordes of city states.

But history has not preserved
    your glorious, envious past,
for warring lords, tyrants of greed,
    have left the world aghast—

Aghast at such destructive greed
    that mind nor beauty trusts,
and for the sake of ego's spoils
    rapes both by its vile lusts.

The modern world has quickly learned
    the story to repeat,
for modern lands warlords replace
    and history too defeat.

But history first is people
    and all that they create.
Destroy the people of a land—
    the worst of any fate!

30. Palmyra

Palmyra, ancient city
    of wealthy caravans
that colonized the Silk Road,
    had monumental plans.

Amorites, Arameans,
    and Arabs were its tribes,
but all spoke Palmyrene
    as wrote its ancient scribes.

Distinctive architecture
    combined from east and west
birthed colonnades and temples,
    a prime artistic quest.

Though wars and many rulers
    destroyed it, then rebuilt,
the richness of its history—
    a multi-colored quilt.

Its art, commerce, religions
    and diverse cultures too
remind us not to forget
    the past in us to view.

We are an image of the past,
    think not that we are new.
Our thoughts, our dreams, others had,
    yes, Palmyrenians too.

Those who destroy Palmyra
    destroy themselves unknown,
for beauty, art dwell in us,
    in us they're flesh and bone.

31. Who Will Dare?

Are you of the opinion
that every Palestinian
    has right to life and land?
Do you take the position
devoid of all contrition:
    They're all a terrorist band?

Are you a faithful Christian
or Jew of disposition
    that God decides all fate?
Should children die of hunger
and every rich warmonger
    spread violence and hate?

Do the Muslims have the right
to see others as a blight
    of infidels on earth?
Will all faiths glibly assume—
on this earth there is no room:
    "Unless you're of my birth?"

Is it providence divine
when I take what's yours as mine
    and murder all my foes?
Does God's will seek to deceive
and us never to relieve
    of dreadful human blows?

Is there peace for humankind
when vile hatred fills the mind
    and is of love devoid?
Who will dare to have the grace
to love all the human race
    till hatred is destroyed?

32. O Die We Must, Yes "Dust to Dust"

O die we must, yes "dust to dust,"
but must we die a death unjust?

When starved in an apartheid scheme
where tyrants' greed cannot redeem,

with policies unjust and shrewd,
and tyrants let them grow no food.

They claim th' oppressed are terror bent
and thus, they are to prison sent.

They have no rights, self to defend;
no help or succor will they lend.

They purge the land, mark owners, fools,
as if there were no moral rules.

The tyrants all their land then rob
as if this were their noblest job!

Others humiliate, condemn—
they only want to tread on them.

Resistance to such acts of greed
is just the pretext that they need

to escalate oppression sure
while claiming their intentions pure.

The tyrant's blood is like th' oppressed
but humanness is unaddressed.

No humanness flows in their veins
to nullify their evil aims.

Merciful Allah, Elohim,
restore with love and peace the dream

to value every person's life
and rid the world of constant strife.

33. Make Peace?

In English "peace" has letters five,
    in French with "paix" there're only four;
in German "Friede" spells with six,
    world languages spell yet with more.

No matter how one spells the word
    few know its meaning, make it real.
Is there a formula for peace?
    Can nations give this word appeal?

Negotiate, reiterate,
    the occupation of the few
who spend their days searching for peace,
    as if the word they never knew.

Without regard and due respect
    for every human being's worth,
negotiations are but play
    and bring no lasting peace on earth.

If there's no will to compromise
    and fairly see another's view,
no sage can help to realize
    a peace that gives to all their due.

34. A Prayer for Peace

We pray for peace, we cry for peace,
    and see the spread of war.
From violence we seek release
    in homelands and afar.
Where children struggle to be fed
    without their parents' care
and have no place to lay their head,
    their faces show despair.

Did Jesus once not say to them,
    "Come, children, come to me?"
Is not the fate of war so grim,
    it seems this cannot be?
All children are not free to go
    when someone bids them come,
when they're confronted by a foe,
    who just destroyed their home.

Do we, peace-lovers, have the will
    to act out what is just?
Will we provide the food and care
    and gain all children's trust?
Will we do what our God commands—
    love friend and foe the same—
feed children with their outstretched hands,
    and honor God's own name?

All violence and war lay waste
    to that which God has made;
they devastate with utmost haste,
    they offer no one aid.
Come once again, O Child of Peace,
    to this destructive earth
that malice, hate, and war may cease;
    give "love for all" new birth.

35. A Plea for Peace

Author of the *songs of earth*
    in every tongue and nation,
you give music, rhythm birth
    and words their inspiration.
You draw music from our soil,
    and every culture's motion,
you shape songs out of our toil,
    the pulse of our emotion.

Author of our *songs of pain*,
    when all our life is aching,
in your music we regain
    our strength when hearts are breaking.
Author of our songs of joy
    that fill us with elation;
you are pain and joy's alloy,
    you are our jubilation.

Author of the *songs of peace*,
    the angels burst forth singing,
when you echoed love's release
    the Christ-child earth was bringing:
"Peace on earth, good will to all"
    is desperately needed;
will we hear this ancient call
    or let it go unheeded?

Author of our *songs of peace*
    in every tongue and nation,
let all hear that wars may cease—
    all hatred, desperation.
Give us songs of peace to sing,
    a global chorus voicing:
"Peace on earth, let freedom ring!"
    Turn suffering to rejoicing!

Section 5

Truth and Justice

36. Justice Remains a Foreign Word

Justice remains a foreign word
    to those who do not care
when needs of poor folk go unheard
    with no desire to share.
Their prime concern is always self;
    immured, they want their way;
the food they've packed on every shelf
    they dare not give away.

The hungry have not worked for bread,
    they have not earned their keep.
Should they by someone else be fed,
    from their abundance reap?
Is it fair to allow the poor
    another's goods to take?
This is no doubt some false *amour,*
    and poor folks "on the make."

Can justice possibly allow
    taking another's food?
This would indeed create a row
    among the wealthy brood!
Their tables laden with the best,
    society's high class
now lazy on their laurels rest—
    contemptible morass!

Who dares claim a human birthright
    that *what is mine is mine*?
Regardless of another's plight
    is this a right divine?
Will you transform this vicious tide
    of greed and apathy
into a swell of genuine pride
    and generous charity?

37. The Prisoner[1]

For years I've sat behind these bars,
    no food received but dirty rice.
No one could come to visit me;
    my mat of straw is filled with lice.

Scarce daylight is there I can see
    through yellowed, tiny window glass;
there is no toilet, just a hole,
    and here I'm forced my days to pass.

What had I done to earn this fate?
    Stood by the road when soldiers came
to take the land my father owned,
    showed them the title with his name.

"Stand back," they said, "or you will pay."
    I said, "We've farmed this land for years."
And then the tall one struck my head.
    I fell, completely filled with fears.

I pleaded still, "Don't take the land!"
    They boldly laughed and bound my hands
and took me to this wretched place,
    and said, "Young man, you've no demands!"

"Demands?" I said, "Just take me home.
    No single thing have I done wrong.
I'm just a boy of fourteen years."
    But here I've been for six years long.

No charge, no trial, no legal help,
    I'm now a man of twenty years,
My family has not heard from me—
    my mother daily sheds her tears.

---

1. Written for Palestinian prisoners on hunger strike.

If now I join a hunger strike
    to fight injustice and this wrong,
I'm judged the worst of criminals,
    but I am weak and they are strong.

If they would look me in the eye
    and say, "Young man, this is unjust.
Can somehow you forgive our crime?"
    I'd have the right to doubt or trust!

38. Is There Hope?

Is there hope for humanity
in a world where insanity,
    not justice, is daily found;
where scorn and rage consume each hour,
the innocence of life devour,
    and love is submerged or drowned?

Stop the rage of persecution
and pursue a resolution
    to end enmity and hate!
Let the prejudice and evil
and the violent upheaval
    of your anger now abate!

39. Equality

No act on earth is more humane
than mothers giving birth;
and no awareness is more sane
than—We're of equal worth!

40. Ethnic Cleansing

An ethnic cleansing, yes, we need
  of every race and tribe!
That washes from the mind with speed
  each hateful diatribe.

How readily one shows the will
  of an ensnaring fiend:
Cultures and lives with hate to kill—
  from hatred never weaned.

Ethnicity, ethnicity—
  Does this say who I am?
Defined with such simplicity,
  it's nothing but a sham.

We're white and yellow, red, black, brown
  with different tongues, faith, dress.
Can we watch others beaten down
  and grant them no redress?

Humanity, humanity—
  this word says who we are.
It takes away our vanity
  and attitudes bizarre.

It underscores our common fate
  to live on planet earth,
to breathe, survive,—the mortal state,
  our destiny from birth.

The commonness of who we are
  is easily ignored,
but mutual love, respect, by far
  surpass life with the sword.

41. The Insanity of Terrorism

With what cruel guile and fury
  do the new fanatics clasp
(as the council, judge, and jury)
  all the terror they can grasp.

For the aged they've no mercy,
  exploit children and the meek.
Spoils of greed have made them pursy
  as they trample on the weak.

Land and homes with rage they plunder,
  ravage all within their path;
even crops are blown asunder
  by the pipe-bombs of their wrath.

What insanity! What terror!
  Thus, they make the foolish claim:
"We are right and you're in error,
  You are wrong and you're to blame."

Who can call such terror justice;
  to plunder, to maim, to kill?
How ludicrous to say, "Trust us"—
  what we do is God's own will?

42. There Are Tables in Our City

There are tables in our city
    filled with lavish food and drink.
Many dine there without pity,
    of the homeless never think.
Would they dare to give them shelter;
    give them food, and clothes to wear?
Much of street life's helter-skelter
    they could change, if they would share.

Who will share a meal-filled table,
    take it out into the street?
Who will help the ones not able;
    give the hungry food to eat?
Who will be the strangers' neighbor,
    hear their agonies and pain?
Side by side who'll share their labor,
    help provide financial gain?

When you hear Christ say, "Come, follow!
    Follow me into the street."
Do not make his promise hollow;
    a full life's no special treat.
It's the promise of the ages
    to all people everywhere.
Even ancient Eastern sages
    with the Christ-child wealth did share.

Feed the hungry, help the helpless,
    give your coat to one in need;
give your life in love that's selfless,
    do a Christ-like, humble deed.
As you open up your living
    to the suffering, stumbling throng,
you'll discover that in giving:
    this transforms the world from wrong.

43. Do Not Steal! (1 Kings 21)

"Naboth, give me your vineyard,"
    bold Ahab dared to say.
His fathers' inheritance
    Naboth could not betray.
So he said "No" to Ahab,
    who thereby was distressed.
But Jezebel his wife said,
    "That vineyard he'll divest!"

She quickly sought to frame him,
    of Naboth some told lies,
with rocks and stones they killed him
    before the people's eyes.
The minute that he heard it,
    brash Ahab claimed his land.
God's dictum, "You shall not steal!"
    he made a fool's command.

This ancient Hebrew story
    repeats itself today.
Ignoring God's commandments,
    the settlers have their way.
Th' inheritance of others
    they disregard and take
land owned by Palestinians;
    they kill, their claims to stake.

This story ends abruptly
    with God's condemning word:
"The dogs will lick the blood of those
    who make God's word absurd."
When you kill and steal the land
    no right you have to own,
God says, "The dogs will lick your blood!"
    Your destiny has flown!

The law God gave on Sinai,
    is it passé today?
"Do not steal and do not kill,"
    has Israel cast away?
How easily they excuse
    such actions with the thought—
The terrorists pursue us
    by them we'll not be caught.

Israel and Palestine,
    awaken your rich past,
for love of others, respect—
    God means for these to last!
Your sacred books still espouse
    these virtues, many more.
To live them will bring justice
    and peace not known before.

44. Truth!

When truth is compromised for gain
and selfish pride one can't restrain,
then truth is what one makes it seem,
and rarely can one truth redeem.
When honesty's a sacrifice,
deception reigns at any price.
The good in humankind is lost,
and lies exact a deadly cost.
They rape the senses and the mind
and make one think others are blind.
They're blind to see they are deceived,
and liars think they've been believed.
But truth has its own simple way
of pointing out those who betray,
betray the truth that's good for all
and cannot hinder their own fall.
Deceivers, hear: "You cannot win,
for truth will take deceivers in!"

45. True or False?

Is there an obscure corner
    within where truth may hide?
Is there some secret venue
    where honesty is tried?

Is tried but yet acquitted
    by plots one has devised:
The soul becomes accomplice
    of truth it has revised?

Deceptive, happy, gay miens
    may cloak dark thoughts beneath.
A smile also may cover
    the gnashing of one's teeth.

How then shall we consider
    those claiming good to do,
when all the time they're trying
    to transform false to true?

46. Free, Simply Free

Refrain:
Free, simply free,
free from all that ever was
that should not be!
Free, simply free,
free to live and laugh and love,
free to be me.
Free, simply free,
free as air and meadows green,
free as the sea.
To be free is what I long for,
to be free is what I live for,
to be free is what I'll die for—
Free, simply free!

Looking back what do I see?—
many things that trouble me:
all the wars that have been fought,
all who lived and died for naught,
friendships lost and gone forever,
all the love that I let sever,
never willing just to live,
never risking to forgive.
I don't want that anymore;
life has so much more in store!
Let me live it full and free,
let me be what I should be.
Refrain

People living everywhere
all have dreams they want to share—
they want shelter, water, food,
they want evil turned to good.
They want children filled with laughter,
free of hate forever after.

They want meaning in their life,
no more violence and strife.
They don't want that anymore;
life has so much more in store!
Let them live it full and free,
let them be what they should be!
Refrain

In the future what will be?
I don't know, for I can't see—
but I know we need on earth
at the moment of each birth
a strong will to love each other
as a sister and a brother.
Stop all hatred, greed, and lust,
turn suspicion into trust!
We want that forevermore;
life has so much more in store!
Let us live it full and free
let us be what we should be!
Refrain

47. Ahav, Agape, Salaam, Shalom

Ahav, agape both mean love;
    they're words from long ago.
Ahav, agape, who will prove
    that these are words they know?
The world is longing for resolve
    but filled with hate and greed.
Where are the folk who seek to solve
    with love what humans need?

The words *salaam, shalom* mean peace;
    O who will give them voice,
that war and violence shall cease?
    It's time to make this choice!
If words for love and peace you know,
    then speak them loud and clear!
Live only love and peace to show,
    and this will banish fear!

Ahav, agape both mean love;
    use them in speech each day.
Salaam, shalom, yes, we can prove
    are words that show the way
to unity, and joy, and peace
    friendship, and a kind word.
So live these words, let love increase
    till hatred is absurd.

Ahav = love in Hebrew
Agape = love in Greek
Shalom = peace in Hebrew
Salaam = peace in Arabic

48. How Shall We See Each Other?

How shall we see each other
    as Muslim, Christian, Jew,
as sister or as brother,
    or as the privileged few?
If there's but one Creator,
    Creator of us all,
no one's the dominator
    before whom others fall.

Is there a human birthright?
    Is there a human race?
Is there a human birth-plight
    that's seen in every face?
What of each human skin hue—
    white, yellow, red, black, brown,
does it show what's within you?
    Should it evoke a frown?

We humans have a history
    that shatters all belief,
and it remains a mystery
    why we act like a thief.
We rob, we steal, and plunder
    the people of our world,
and then we stand in wonder
    when hatred is unfurled.

Can we be as created,
    be as we're meant to be,
with prejudice abated,
    one earthly family?
Can we respect our neighbor
    of different culture, creed,
and for each other labor,
    no matter what the need?

Can we speak of humankind,
    one people of the earth,
people not of single mind,
    yet bound by human birth?
Can we find a way to say,
    "By love I'll live and move;
love will guide my words each day,
    my actions it will prove"?

It's time we learned in living
    that all on earth are blessed
with inner strength for giving,
    a gift not oft assessed.
We can give to each other
    the love that's in our soul.
How tragic love to smother,
    for love makes humans whole!

49. The Politics of Waiting

The politics of waiting,
    the tactics of delay,
result in deaths and anguish;
    for children die each day.

How much longer shall we wait
    for Jews' and Arabs' peace?
Is the delay a tactic,
    that now will never cease?

Tactics as a brutal art
    destroy both hope and truth,
ending possibility,
    like some malignant sleuth.

Israel waits and waits and waits,
    the Palestinians too!
Such useless, senseless waiting
    the world must *now* eschew!

50. Hope Against Hope

Homage to wealth, and rank, and power
the world escapes no single hour.
Forced to submit, as slaves to cower,
the rich the poor as prey devour.

From land to land it is the same,
as starved-marked faces bear the shame.
The power-hungry crush the weak,
even when they justice claim to seek.

Beware lest ire from sleep awake
and power from the powerful take.
If I were in a gentler mood,
perhaps I'd be more wise and good.

But where there's evil in this life,
I'm not a spectator of strife!
Sit by while no one says a word?
Then life would surely be absurd!

I will not be mere bard or sage,
or make of history a blank page.
The written word or lyric wise
must speak the truth, not be its guise.

The battles that are won by wrong
oft make the weak, downtrodden strong,
expose the vile and inhumane
till wisdom, truth make humans sane.

O God, let justice rule and reign,
remove oppression, woe, and pain.
Give us the strength to intervene,
for without hope we oft have been.

Though greed and malice are well known,
atonement's made by love alone.
Amends and reparations make?
Indeed! for humankind's own sake!

www.ingramcontent.com/pod-product-compliance
Lightning Source LLC
Chambersburg PA
CBHW071105090426
42737CB00013B/2488